In the river, hidden under a rock, sits a crab. He is looking out for some food.

He sees a floating scrap of fish,
and nip! He grabs it.

The fish floats up, with the crab hanging on to it.

Up, up, up floats the crab with the scrap of fish.

Then, suddenly, the crab is not in the river at all.

He is not floating.
He is dangling from some string.

"Get him, get him!" the children shout. "Do not let him drop back into the river."

The crab is dropped, not into the
river but into a net.

From the net he can see a bucket, with lots of crabs clambering about in it.

The crab is added to the bucket.
"We did it!" yell the children.
"We are the winners!"

"We were the quickest to catch a hundred crabs!" they shout, jumping about.

Then the children empty the
bucket of crabs.

The crabs all scatter and run
along the muddy river bank.

Back in the river, hidden under a rock, sits the crab. He is looking out for some food.